cheesecakes

RYLAND
PETERS
& SMALL
LONDON NEW YORK

cheesecakes

Maxine Clark   Photography by Martin Brigdale

First published in the USA in 2003
Ryland Peters & Small, Inc.
519 Broadway, 5th Floor
New York, NY 10012
www.rylandpeters.com

10 9 8 7 6 5 4 3 2 1

Text © Maxine Clark 2003
Design and photographs
© Ryland Peters & Small 2003

Printed in China

Library of Congress Cataloging-in-
Publication Data

Clark, Maxine.
  Cheesecakes / Maxine Clark ;
photography by Martin Brigdale.
      p. cm.
  ISBN 1-84172-488-2
  1. Cheesecake (Cookery) I. Title.
  TX773 .C563 2003
  641.8'653--dc21
                        2003004010

Senior Designer Steve Painter
Commissioning Editor
Elsa Petersen-Schepelern
Editors Kathy Steer, Susan Stuck
Production Patricia Harrington
Art Director Gabriella Le Grazie
Publishing Director Alison Starling

Food Stylists Maxine Clark,
Bridget Sargeson
Stylist Helen Trent
Indexer Hilary Bird

Author's acknowledgments
Special thanks go to my sister Jacks
for help with recipe testing. Thanks
to Martin and Helen for producing
wonderful photographs yet again,
with Bridget, who will probably never eat
a cheesecake again. My lovely editor,
Elsa, should get any blame for weight
gain when using this book—
it was her idea.

Notes
• All spoon measurements are level
unless otherwise specified.
• All eggs are large unless otherwise
specified. Uncooked or partially cooked
eggs should not be served to the very
young, the very old, those with
compromised immune systems, or to
pregnant women.
• Before baking, weigh or measure all
ingredients exactly and prepare baking
pans or trays.
• Ovens should be preheated to the
specified temperature. Recipes in this
book were tested in several kinds of
oven—all work slightly differently. I
recommend using an oven thermometer
and consulting the maker's handbook for
special instructions.

**Fat content of cheeses
used in this book**

All cheeses labeled "Light" or "Extra-
Light" have added stabilizers, and
although they reduce the calories, the
texture in cooked cheesecakes may be
different when substituted for the higher
fat version.

• Cottage Cheese (white, with a
knobbly texture and slight acidity) has
4 percent fat.
• Ricotta (made from the recooked
whey left over from making cheese) is
white, with a slightly granular texture—
12 percent fat.
• Philadelphia Full Fat Soft Cheese (white
and creamy smooth) has 15 percent fat.
• Mascarpone (an Italian cream cheese,
pale yellow and creamy, with a distinctive
rich creamy flavor) has 20 percent fat.

contents

delightful desserts ...

Say the word "cheesecake" and most people will sigh with pleasure and start to recall their favorites. We see cheesecakes everywhere now, from coffee bars to supermarket shelves, but the best are always homemade.

My first taste of a real baked cheesecake was on trips to Harrogate in Yorkshire many years ago. They were thick and dense and incredibly rich. Then I tasted real Jewish cheesecake in Petticoat Lane in London—this was a revelation! I was converted, and started to collect and try all sorts of recipes. Cheesecake was particularly popular in Britain in the '70s, and always seen as something rather exotic—it came from faraway places like Italy, America, and Eastern Europe. In America of course, immigrants from all over the world contributed their own twist to the art, whether it be the type of cheese used, or the added ingredients.

That said, baked cheesecake is always best served with coffee. Nowadays, we forget that these baked cheesecakes came earlier than the lighter cheesecakes set with gelatin, which were seen as a quick and easy alternative, and could look very glamorous indeed. Gelatin-set cheesecakes were the perfect conclusion to a dinner party and still are today—they look spectacular, are relatively simple to make, and taste wonderful. Whether baked or set, cheesecakes are a firm favorite in the Western world, and the best are made at home, especially if it's one of these ...

making cheesecake bases
shortcrust dough

This is the classic method for making short and crumbly shortcrust dough. It is made with half butter and half lard—the butter for color and flavor and the cooking fat for shortness. If you have cool hands, the hand method is best as it will incorporate more air than in a food processor. If you have hot hands, the food processor is a blessing! The quantities of water added vary according to the humidity of the flour—always add less than it says, you can always add more if it is dry, but once it is a sticky mess, it could prove disastrous!

basic shortcrust dough

1⅔ cups all-purpose flour, plus
extra for dusting

a pinch of salt

⅓ cup chilled lard or shortening,
in small pieces

6 tablespoons chilled unsalted
butter, cut into small pieces

2–3 tablespoons cold water

**Makes about 14 oz., enough to
line the base of a 9-inch fluted
flan pan, or 10 false-bottom
tartlet pans, 4 inches diameter**

Sift the flour and salt into a large bowl. Add the lard
and butter, and using your fingertips, rub it in until
the mixture resembles fine bread crumbs. Stir in
enough cold water, about 2–3 tablespoons, to
produce a firm dough.

Transfer the dough to a lightly floured work surface
and knead lightly. Shape the dough into a flattened
ball, wrap in plastic wrap, and chill for at least
30 minutes before rolling out.

To make the dough in a food processor, sift the flour
and salt into the processor. Add the lard and butter
and process for 30 seconds until the mixture
resembles very fine bread crumbs. Pour in
2 tablespoons cold water and pulse for 10 seconds.
The dough should start to come together in large
lumps. If not, add 1 tablespoon water and pulse
again. As soon as the dough forms a large lump,
transfer to a lightly floured work surface and knead
lightly. Proceed as above.

Note for both recipes If using a food processor, do
not overprocess, otherwise the dough will be tough.

rich shortcrust dough

1⅔ cups all-purpose flour, plus
extra for dusting

½ teaspoon salt

1 stick chilled unsalted butter,
cut into small pieces

2 egg yolks

2–3 tablespoons cold water

**Makes about 14 oz., enough to
line the base of a 9-inch fluted
flan pan, or 10 false-bottom
tartlet pans, 4 inches diameter**

Sift the flour and salt into a large bowl. Add the
butter and, using your fingertips, rub it in until the
mixture resembles fine bread crumbs. Stir in the egg
yolks mixed with at least 2 tablespoons cold water
to make a firm but malleable dough.

Transfer the dough to a lightly floured work surface
and knead until smooth. Shape the dough into a
flattened ball, wrap in plastic wrap, and chill for at
least 30 minutes before rolling out.

To make the dough in a food processor, sift the flour
and salt into the processor. Add the butter and
process for 30 seconds until the mixture resembles
fine bread crumbs. Pour in the egg yolks mixed with
at least 2 tablespoons cold water and pulse for
10 seconds. The dough should start to come together
in lumps. If not, add 1 tablespoon water and pulse
again. As soon as the dough forms a large lump, tip
out onto a lightly floured work surface and knead
into a firm but malleable dough. Proceed as above.

Variation To make Sweet Rich Shortcrust Dough,
add 2 tablespoons confectioners' sugar with the flour.

cookie bases

cookie crumb base

8 oz. graham crackers

4 tablespoons unsalted butter

¼ cup sugar

Makes enough to line the base of an 8-inch pan or dish

Put the cookies in a food processor and blend until crumbs form. Alternatively, put the cookies in a plastic bag and crush finely with a rolling pin.

Melt the butter and sugar in a small saucepan over gentle heat. Stir in the crumbs and use at once.

chocolate crumb base

8 oz. chocolate-coated cookies or chocolate chip cookies

6 tablespoons unsalted butter

2 tablespoons brown sugar

Makes enough to line the base of an 8-inch pan or dish

Put the cookies in a food processor and blend until crumbs form. Alternatively, put the cookies into a plastic bag and crush finely with a rolling pin.

Melt the butter and sugar in a small saucepan over gentle heat. Stir in the crumbs and use at once.

nutty cookie crumb base

3 oz. graham crackers

4 tablespoons unsalted butter

¼ cup sugar

1 tablespoon chopped toasted nuts, such as hazelnuts, walnuts or almonds, about 1 oz.

Makes enough to line the base of an 8 inch pan or dish

Put the crackers into a food processor and blend until crumbs form. Alternatively, put the cookies into a plastic bag and crush finely with a rolling pin.

Melt the butter and sugar in a small saucepan over gentle heat. Stir in the crumbs and chopped nuts and use at once.

Note To toast nuts, put them in a dry skillet and stir over gentle heat until starting to color all over. Watch them closely, because they burn easily. Alternatively, spread the nuts in a baking pan and cook in a preheated oven at 375°F until lightly colored.

oven-baked cheesecakes

Baked cheesecake mixtures contain whole eggs, which add
lightness to the mixture and cook to set the cake. Classic American
and Italian cheesecakes are made this way and have a completely
different texture from a set cheesecake. Some are deep and some
shallow, but both have a tendency to crack during cooking, so don't
worry if this happens to you.

This is the real thing—a dense, rich cheesecake with a crunchy cookie base. Serve with coffee.

traditional new york cheesecake

Base

8 oz. graham crackers

1 stick unsalted butter

¼ cup plus 2 tablespoons sugar

Filling

1½ sticks unsalted butter

¾ cup sugar

4 extra-large eggs, beaten

3 tablespoons all-purpose flour

finely grated zest and juice of 1 large unwaxed lemon

½ teaspoon vanilla extract

3 packages cream cheese, 8 oz. each, at room temperature

¼ cup milk

Topping

1¾ cups sour cream

1 tablespoon confectioners' sugar

freshly squeezed juice of 1 lemon

a springform cake pan, 9 inches diameter, greased

a baking sheet with sides

To make the crumb base, put the cookies into a food processor and blend until fine crumbs form. Alternatively, put the cookies in a large plastic bag and finely crush them with a rolling pin. Melt the butter in a small saucepan over gentle heat, then stir in the crumbs and sugar. Spread the crumb mixture over the base of the prepared cake pan, pressing down lightly. Set the pan on a baking sheet with sides and bake in a preheated oven at 375°F for 8–10 minutes. Remove from the oven and let cool.

Reduce the temperature to 325°F. To make the filling, put the butter and sugar in a large bowl and, using a wooden spoon or electric hand mixer, beat until pale and fluffy. Gradually beat in the eggs. Mix in the flour, lemon zest, lemon juice, and vanilla. Put the cream cheese in a separate bowl and, using a wooden spoon or electric hand mixer, beat until smooth. Gently beat in the milk, then gradually beat in the butter and sugar mixture. Spoon the mixture onto the crumb base and level the surface. Bake for 1½ hours.

To make the topping, put the sour cream, confectioners' sugar, and lemon juice in a large bowl and, using a wooden spoon or electric hand mixer, beat lightly. Chill in the refrigerator until required.

Remove the cheesecake from the oven and increase the temperature to 375°F. Pour the topping over the surface of the cheesecake, level, and return to the preheated oven for a further 10 minutes or until set. Turn off the oven, leave the door ajar, and let the cheesecake cool in the oven to prevent it cracking. Alternatively, transfer it to a wire rack, invert a large bowl over the cake, then let cool. Chill the cheesecake for at least 6 hours before serving.

I have been making this cheesecake since I started cooking, at the tender age of eight—it used to be my *pièce de résistance*! Blending the sugar with large strips of lemon zest transfers all the essential oils to the sugar and gives a wonderful aroma to the tart. Use cottage cheese instead of cream cheese to give a lighter texture to the cake. Mascarpone Cream or Lemon Syllabub Cream (page 63) would be delicious with this cheesecake.

simple lemon cheesecake

1 recipe Sweet Rich Shortcrust Dough (page 9, see Variation), at room temperature

all-purpose flour, for dusting

Filling

1 unwaxed lemon

⅓ cup sugar

1½ packages cream cheese, 12 oz.

1 large egg, plus 3 egg yolks

2 teaspoons vanilla extract

a false-bottom tart pan, 9 inches diameter

parchment paper and ceramic baking beans or rice or foil

Serves 6–8

Roll out the dough on a lightly floured work surface and use to line the tart pan. Prick the base with a fork, then chill or freeze for 15 minutes. Cut out a large piece of parchment paper to fit the pan, use to line the cheesecake crust, then fill with ceramic baking beans or rice. Alternatively, line the cheesecake crust with crumpled foil. Bake in a preheated oven at 375°F for 10 minutes. Remove the parchment paper and beans or foil and return to the oven for a further 10 minutes. Set the crust aside to cool; leave the oven on.

Using a vegetable peeler, remove the zest from the lemon leaving behind any white pith, then squeeze the juice. Put the lemon zest and sugar in a food processor or blender and blend until the sugar and lemon zest mixture looks damp.

Add the lemon juice and blend again—the lemon zest should have completely dissolved in the sugar—then add the cream cheese, the whole egg, egg yolks, and vanilla extract and blend until smooth. Pour the mixture into the cheesecake crust.

Bake the cheesecake for 25 minutes or until just set and lightly browned on top. Remove from the oven and let cool. Serve at room temperature.

Pastry

1½ cups fine polenta or cornmeal

½ cup all-purpose flour, plus extra for dusting

½ cup plus 2 tablespoons sugar

½ cup toasted pine nuts, 2 oz.

1¾ sticks unsalted butter, diced

2 extra-large egg yolks

Ricotta and Raisin Filling

2–3 tablespoons Vin Santo or Marsala wine

½ cup large raisins, preferably muscatel, about 3 oz.

1 lb. fresh ricotta cheese, about 2 cups

2 packages cream cheese, such as Philadelphia, 8 oz. each

1 cup sour cream

4 large eggs, separated

⅔ cup sugar

2 teaspoons vanilla extract

a large pinch of salt

freshly grated nutmeg

a springform cake pan, 10 inches diameter, lined with nonstick parchment paper, the sides greased with butter

baking parchment and ceramic baking beans or rice or foil

Serves 8–10

Delicious for a summer lunch, this rich cheesecake is perfect for any special occasion. For best results, make sure all the filling ingredients are at room temperature.

ricotta and raisin cheesecake

To make the dough, put the polenta, flour, sugar, pine nuts, and butter in a food processor and blend, in short bursts, until the mixture resembles coarse bread crumbs. Add the egg yolks and process until the dough forms a ball. Wrap in plastic wrap and chill for 1 hour.

Roll out the dough on a piece of lightly floured, wax paper to ¼ inch thick and carefully use to line the pan. Chill for 5 minutes. Cut out a large piece of parchment paper to fit the pan, set on top of the pastry dough, then fill with ceramic baking beans or rice. Alternatively, line the pastry dough with crumpled foil. Bake in a preheated oven at 350°F for 10 minutes. Remove the parchment paper and beans or foil and return to the oven for a further 10 minutes. Set the crust aside to cool; leave the oven on.

To make the filling, pour the Vin Santo or Marsala over the raisins, mix well, and leave to plump up for a few hours or overnight. (You can speed this up by heating them for a minute in the microwave.)

Put the ricotta, cream cheese, and sour cream in a bowl and beat with a wooden spoon. Put the egg yolks and sugar in a separate bowl and beat with an electric hand mixer until light and creamy. Add the cheese mixture and vanilla and beat until smooth.

Put the egg whites and a pinch of salt in a separate bowl and beat until soft peaks form. Fold the beaten egg whites into the cheese mixture, then spoon into the cold cheesecake crust. Sprinkle freshly grated nutmeg generously over the top.

Bake in the center of the oven for 30–40 minutes or until golden but still a little soft in the middle (it will continue to cook after removing from the oven). Let cool on a wire rack. (Many cheesecakes split when baking, but don't worry if it has—the split will contract as it cools.) As with all cheesecakes, serve at room temperature, not chilled.

This is a delicious and simple cheesecake made in my grandfather's native county. Although he married a Scots lass and lived all his married life in Scotland, he still ate his apple pie or Christmas pudding with a wedge of cheese like a true Yorkshireman. He would have loved this cheesecake.

yorkshire cheesecake

½ recipe Basic Shortcrust Dough (page 9)

all-purpose flour, for dusting

Filling

8 oz. cottage cheese, 1 cup

2 tablespoons sugar

2 large eggs

finely grated zest of 1½ unwaxed lemons and the juice of ½ lemon

2 teaspoons cornstarch

2 tablespoons heavy cream

1 tablespoon melted butter

2 oz. raisins or currants, soaked in boiling water for 20 minutes

a deep pie plate or false-bottom tart pan, 10 inches diameter

parchment paper and ceramic baking beans or rice or foil

Serves 6

Roll out the dough thinly on a lightly floured work surface and use to line the pie plate or tart pan. Chill or freeze for 20 minutes. If using a pie plate, make a decorative edge. Cut out a piece of parchment paper to fit the plate or pan and set on the dough, then fill with ceramic baking beans or rice. Alternatively, line the dough with crumpled foil. Bake in a preheated oven at 400°F for 10 minutes. Remove the parchment paper and beans or foil and return to the oven for a further 5 minutes. Reduce the oven temperature to 350°F.

Press the cottage cheese through a fine-mesh sieve into a large bowl. Add the sugar, eggs, lemon zest, and lemon juice and, using a wooden spoon or electric hand mixer, beat until smooth. Put the cornstarch and cream in another bowl, mix to a smooth paste, then beat into the cheese mixture with the melted butter. Pour the mixture into the dough-lined pan.

Drain the raisins, pat dry with paper towels, then sprinkle them over the top of the cheesecake. Bake for 30 minutes until set. Let cool and serve at cool room temperature.

These were named after the ladies (maids of honor) who carried them back to Richmond Palace for King Henry VIII or Queen Elizabeth I—both monarchs, it is said, loved these little cheesecakes made by a local baker. I include a spoonful of best cherry preserves in the base of each—almond and cherry make a great combination. I like to make these in small deep pans (like mini-brioche pans) if you can find them, because the filling seems moister and they look great!

little richmond maids of honor

1 recipe Sweet Rich Shortcrust Dough (page 9, see Variation), at room temperature

all-purpose flour, for dusting

Filling

½ stick unsalted butter

¼ cup plus 2 tablespoons sugar

finely grated zest and juice of 1 unwaxed lemon

4 oz. cottage cheese, ½ cup

2 extra-large eggs, beaten

⅓ cup brandy or cherry brandy

4 oz. slivered almonds, crushed to a powder, or ground almonds

about ¾ cup cherry conserve

8 small sprigs of rosemary (optional)

salt

confectioners' sugar, for dusting

8 false-bottom tartlet pans, 4 inches diameter*

Makes 8

Roll out the dough thinly on a lightly floured work surface and use to line the base and sides of the pans. Chill for 30 minutes.

Put the butter, sugar, and lemon zest in a large bowl and, using a wooden spoon or electric hand mixer, beat until pale and fluffy. Press the cottage cheese through a fine-mesh sieve into another bowl (do not blend in a food processor, otherwise the texture will be altered), then beat the cheese into the butter and sugar mixture. Beat in the eggs, lemon juice, and brandy, then gently fold in the ground almonds and a pinch of salt.

Drop a spoonful of cherry conserve into each cheesecake crust and spoon the almond filling on top, about two-thirds full to allow for rising. Bake in a preheated oven at 350°F for 20–25 minutes until risen and golden brown. Remove from the oven and let cool slightly. Spear each one with a sprig of rosemary, if using, and serve warm, dusted with confectioners' sugar.

Note These cheesecakes can also be made in smaller, deeper pans, but will need a longer cooking time.

goat cheese and ginger cheesecake with rhubarb compote

Dough

2⅓ cups all-purpose flour, plus extra for dusting

2 sticks unsalted butter

2 teaspoons ground ginger

2 tablespoons confectioners' sugar, sifted

1 extra-large egg, beaten

⅓ cup chilled sweet white wine mixed with 2 tablespoons very finely chopped candied ginger

salt

Filling

1 lb. soft goat cheese

½ cup sugar

vanilla extract, to taste

6 extra-large eggs, separated

⅔ cup heavy cream

4 oz. chopped preserved ginger or chopped candied ginger

12–15 fresh bay leaves, to decorate (optional)

Rhubarb Compote

2 lb. fresh rhubarb, trimmed

1¾ cups sugar, or to taste

a springform cake pan, 9 inches diameter

Serves 10

This deep, creamy, mild cheesecake made with goat cheese is spectacular when served with a stunningly pink compote of new season's rhubarb. Because rhubarb and ginger are such a classic flavor combination, I've added ginger to the dough as well as the filling to give it a bit of punch!

To make the dough, put the flour in a large bowl, add the butter, and rub it in until the mixture resembles bread crumbs. Add the ginger, sugar, salt, egg, and wine and mix to a firm dough. Transfer the dough to a lightly floured work surface and knead lightly, then wrap and chill for 30 minutes. Roll out the dough thinly on a lightly floured work surface and use to line the cake pan. Chill or freeze for 15 minutes, then trim down ¾ inch from the top edge of the pan and discard the trimmings. Chill until required.

Put the goat cheese, sugar, vanilla extract, egg yolks, and cream in a large bowl and, using a wooden spoon or electric hand mixer, beat lightly. Stir in the chopped ginger. Put 4 of the egg whites and a pinch of salt in a spotlessly clean, grease-free bowl and beat until stiff but not dry. Fold into the cheese mixture, then spoon into the cheesecake crust. Decorate with a ring of bay leaves (do this lightly because they will sink slightly during cooking). Bake in a preheated oven at 350°F for 20 minutes, then cover the top with foil (to prevent the bay leaves from burning) and bake for a further 25 minutes or until well-risen and dark golden brown. Turn off the oven, uncover the cheesecake, and let cool in the oven for 20 minutes. Serve warm or room temperature (not chilled) with the compote.

To make the compote, cut the rhubarb into 1-inch chunks and put in a wide saucepan. Add the sugar, cover, and cook, stirring occasionally, for 10 minutes or until the juices start to flow, the rhubarb starts to disintegrate, and the sugar dissolves. Taste and add more sugar if necessary. Transfer to a bowl to cool, cover with plastic wrap, and chill until required.

I first tasted this cheesecake on a trip to France, when luscious, ripe, red-centered figs were in season at the end of September. The contrast between the plain light vanilla cheesecake, crisp crust, and warm, caramelized figs was a revelation!

caramelized purple fig cheesecake

1 recipe Sweet Rich Shortcrust Dough (page 9, see Variation), at room temperature

all-purpose flour, for dusting

Filling

3 large eggs

1 stick unsalted butter, softened

½ cup plus 2 tablespoons sugar or vanilla sugar

1 package cream cheese, 8 oz.

1 vanilla bean

8 ripe purple figs (the ones with the ruby red centers)

red currant jelly

salt

a false-bottom tart pan, 8 inches diameter

parchment paper and ceramic baking beans or rice or foil

Serves 6

Roll out the dough thinly on a lightly floured work surface and use to line the tart pan. Prick the base with a fork. Cut out a large piece of parchment paper to fit the pan and set in the dough-lined pan, then fill with ceramic baking beans or rice. Alternatively, line with crumpled foil. Bake in a preheated oven at 375°F for 10 minutes. Remove the parchment paper and beans or foil and return to the oven for a further 5 minutes or until just colored. Put 1 egg and a pinch of salt in a small bowl and beat well, then use to brush the inside of the baked cheesecake crust. Bake for a further 5–8 minutes until the egg is set and shiny. Set the crust aside to cool; leave the oven on.

Put the butter and sugar in a large bowl and, using a wooden spoon or electric hand mixer, beat until soft and fluffy, then beat in the soft cheese. Split the vanilla bean and scrape out the seeds with the tip of a knife. Put the 2 remaining eggs in a separate bowl, add the vanilla seeds, and beat well, then gradually beat them into the cheese mixture. Pour the filling into the cheesecake crust and bake for 25–30 minutes until risen and brown. Let cool in the pan for 10 minutes, then transfer to a wire rack to cool completely.

Cut the figs into quarters and arrange on top of the cheesecake, making sure that they sit upright. Put the red currant jelly in a small saucepan, warm over gentle heat, then lightly brush over the figs. Cover the dough edges with foil to prevent overbrowning. Put the cheesecake under a preheated broiler and cook quickly until the figs start to bubble and brown. Brush with some more warm red currant jelly and serve immediately.

When I first visited Salzburg in Austria, I was amazed by the variety of sweet cakes and pastries on display. I had never seen such a variety of strudels—all shapes and sizes, flavors, and textures. This was one of my favorites. If fresh cherries are not available, use frozen ones, but drain them well before adding to the filling.

cottage cheese and cherry strudels

12 sheets phyllo dough

1 stick unsalted butter, melted

confectioners' sugar, for dusting

Filling

6 tablespoons butter

5 tablespoons sugar

2 large eggs, separated

8 oz. cottage cheese, 1 cup, strained*

finely grated zest of
1 unwaxed lemon

½ teaspoon ground cinnamon

¼ cup sour cream

8 oz. fresh cherries, pitted and quartered

several large baking sheets, lightly oiled

Makes about 12

To make the filling, put the butter and sugar in a large bowl and, using a wooden spoon or electric hand mixer, beat until pale and fluffy. Stir in the egg yolks, strained cottage cheese, lemon zest, cinnamon, and sour cream, then fold in the cherries. Put the egg whites in a separate spotlessly clean, grease-free bowl and beat until stiff with an electric hand mixer or balloon whisk. Gently fold into the cheese mixture.

Keep the phyllo dough sheets covered with plastic wrap to prevent them drying out. Put a phyllo dough sheet on a clean work surface and brush with a little melted butter. Starting at the short side of each sheet of dough, 1 inch in from the front edge, spoon about 2 heaping tablespoons of the mixture along the edge, keeping 1 inch in from the sides. Flip the bottom edge over the filling, roll once, then flip the sides inwards to encase the filling completely. Roll up like a cigar, brush with melted butter, and set on a large baking tray. Repeat with the other sheets of dough.

Bake in a preheated oven at 375°F for about 20 minutes, until the dough is firm and golden brown. Let cool slightly, then dust with confectioners' sugar and serve warm.

*Note If you make the filling with an electric mixer, the cottage cheese won't have to be strained.

This is a very special cheesecake indeed. Make sure that the chocolate and water melt together—the shock of adding the water later will make the chocolate thicken and set into a lump.

chocolate marble cheesecake

1 recipe Chocolate Crumb Crust (page 10)

a little melted butter

4 oz. white chocolate, grated and chilled, to decorate

Filling

6 oz. bittersweet chocolate, chopped

3 packages cream cheese, 8 oz. each, at room temperature

1¼ cups sugar

1 vanilla bean, split, seeds scraped out and set aside, or 1 teaspoon vanilla extract

2 extra-large eggs

a springform cake pan or deep cake pan with a removable base, 9 inches diameter

Serves 10

Press the chocolate crumb crust mixture into the base of the cake pan and bake in a preheated oven at 350°F for 15 minutes. Remove from the oven, lightly firm down again, and let cool completely. Reduce the oven temperature to 325°F.

When the base is cold, carefully paint the sides of the pan with a little melted butter, then chill until required. Put the bittersweet chocolate and 2 tablespoons water in a small heatproof bowl set over a saucepan of barely simmering water. Stir occasionally until the chocolate is melted and smooth, then keep it warm.

Put the cream cheese, sugar, and vanilla seeds, if using, in a large bowl and, using a wooden spoon or electric hand mixer, beat until soft and creamy. Put the eggs and vanilla extract, if using, in a bowl and beat well. Gradually beat the eggs into the cheese mixture. Pour 1 cup of the mixture into a small pitcher, then pour the remaining mixture into the prepared pan.

Stir the warm chocolate into the reserved cheese mixture. Pour the chocolate mixture in a wide zigzag pattern over the surface of the cheesecake, edge to edge. Draw the handle of a thick wooden spoon through the pattern, zigzagging in the opposite way so the mixtures are marbled together. Do not overwork, or the pattern will be lost. Keep it simple and the edges neat.

Bake for 20–25 minutes, or until the cheesecake starts to puff slightly around the edges but is still very soft in the center. Carefully transfer the cake to a wire rack and loosen the edges with a very thin knife blade. Let cool slowly by setting a large upturned bowl over the cheesecake. When completely cold, chill for at least 3 hours before removing the pan. Remove the pan and spread the sides lightly with a very thin layer of whipped cream. Press the grated white chocolate around the sides. Cut with a hot knife to serve.

An outrageously rich cheesecake based on the delicious ingredients of *tiramisù*—coffee, mascarpone, chocolate, coffee liqueur, and rum. A creamy rum and vanilla combination is marbled through a plain chocolate, coffee and liqueur mixture, poured into an amaretti crust, and baked.

tiramisù cheesecake

Base

10 oz. amaretti cookies
or macaroons

6 tablespoons unsalted butter

confectioners' sugar, for dusting
(optional)

Filling

1½ lb. mascarpone or cream
cheese, at room temperature

¾ cup sugar

3 large eggs, separated

3 tablespoons all-purpose flour

2 tablespoons dark rum

½ teaspoon vanilla extract

7 oz. bittersweet chocolate

1 tablespoon finely ground
espresso coffee

3 tablespoons coffee liqueur, such
as Tía María

*a springform cake pan,
9 inches diameter*

Serves 8–10

Put the cookies in a blender or food processor and blend until finely ground. Alternatively, put the cookies in a large plastic bag and crush with a rolling pin. Put the butter in a saucepan and heat gently until melted, then stir into the crumbs until they are well coated. Spoon into the cake pan and, using the back of a spoon, press evenly over the base and 1¾ inches up the sides to form a neat shell. Chill in the refrigerator for at least 30 minutes until firm.

Put the mascarpone or cream cheese in a large bowl and, using a wooden spoon or electric hand mixer, beat until smooth. Add the sugar and beat until smooth, then beat in the egg yolks. Divide the mixture in half and put into 2 bowls. Stir the flour, rum, and vanilla extract into one of the bowls.

Put the chocolate in a small heatproof bowl set over a saucepan of simmering water and melt gently. Let cool slightly, then stir in the coffee and coffee liqueur. Stir into the second bowl. Put the egg whites in a spotlessly clean, grease-free bowl, beat until soft peaks form, then fold half into each flavored cheese mixture.

Quickly spoon alternate mounds of the cheese mixture into the cheesecake base until full. Swirl the mixtures together with a knife to produce a marbled effect (do not overmix). Bake in a preheated oven at 400°F for 45 minutes until golden brown, but still soft in the center—cover the top if it appears to be overbrowning. Turn off the oven, leave the door ajar, and let the cheesecake cool in the oven to prevent it cracking. Alternatively, transfer the cheesecake to a wire rack and invert a large bowl over the cake so it cools slowly. When cold, chill for several hours before serving. Serve dusted with confectioners' sugar, if using.

lanched hazelnuts,

r̶a̶ sauce (page 63),
to serve

Filling

1 cup sugar

4 tablespoons unsalted butter,
softened

2 packages cream cheese, 8 oz.
each, at room temperature

2½ tablespoons all-purpose flour

2 tablespoons honey

5 large eggs, separated

¼ cup plus 2 tablespoons light
cream

1 teaspoon vanilla extract

½ teaspoon ground cinnamon

½ teaspoon grated nutmeg

¼ cup brown sugar

3 oz. hazelnuts, toasted, skins
rubbed off, and coarsely chopped

a large baking sheet, oiled

*a springform cake pan, 10 inches
diameter, greased and floured*

Serves 10

I used to make this for big parties—easy to prepare in advance
and utterly delicious. Don't use a honey that is too strong or it
will dominate the flavor—acacia or orange blossom is just fine.

honey hazelnut crunch cheesecake

To make the praline, put the hazelnuts and sugar in a saucepan and set
over gentle heat until the sugar has melted. Do not stir.

When melted, increase the heat and boil until the melted sugar turns to
golden caramel. Immediately pour onto an oiled baking sheet and let set
and cool completely—about 1 hour. Break up into pieces, then put into a
blender or food processor and grind to a fine powder. Store in an airtight
jar until required.

To make the filling, put the sugar and butter in a large bowl and, using a
wooden spoon or electric hand mixer, beat until pale and fluffy. Add the
cream cheese and beat until fluffy. Beat in the flour, honey, and egg yolks.
Stir in the cream, vanilla extract, spices, and half the praline.

Put the egg whites in a separate spotlessly clean, grease-free bowl and
beat until stiff peaks form. Gently fold into the cheese mixture, then pour
into the prepared cake pan.

Put the brown sugar in a bowl, stir in the chopped hazelnuts, then sprinkle
over the surface of the cheesecake. Bake in a preheated oven at 325°F for
1 hour, then turn off the oven, leave the door ajar, and let the cheesecake
cool in the oven for about 2 hours to prevent it cracking. Alternatively,
transfer the cheesecake to a wire rack and invert a large bowl over the
cake so it cools slowly. Chill for 2 hours, but serve at room temperature
sprinkled with the remaining hazelnut praline. Serve with raspberry sauce.

icebox cheesecakes

Uncooked cheesecake mixtures are flavored in various ways and set with gelatin. The mixture is usually poured into a prepared crust or onto a base of some description, usually made from crushed cookie or cracker crumbs mixed with melted butter. Sometimes ladyfingers are used for a lighter effect. The flavors and textures are limitless, but a light hand is needed when beating and folding in egg whites for an airy texture. Most fillings are lightly set, because too much gelatin can give a rubbery texture.

Loosely based on the mixture for Italian *panna cotta*, these silky smooth cheesecakes are easy to make, yet very sophisticated. If you can't buy mascarpone, use heavy cream instead. The cream will be less rich but still delicious.

mascarpone biscotti cheesecakes

2 recipes Cookie Crumb Base (page 10), made with Italian biscotti (cantuccini)

Filling

1¼ cups mascarpone, at room temperature

1¼ cups heavy cream

thinly peeled zest of 1 unwaxed orange

½ cup plus 2 tablespoons sugar

1 vanilla bean, split lengthwise

¼ cup milk

1 tablespoon powdered gelatin

6 false-bottom tartlet pans, 4 inches diameter

a baking sheet with sides

Serves 6

Press the crumb mixture neatly into the base and sides of the tartlet pans. Set on a baking sheet with sides and chill until required.

Put the mascarpone in a large bowl and, using a wooden spoon or electric hand mixer, beat until softened.

Put the cream, orange zest, sugar, and vanilla bean in a medium saucepan and heat until almost but not quite boiling. Stir occasionally to loosen the vanilla seeds from the bean. Remove from the heat and leave to infuse for 20 minutes. When cooled, remove the bean and gradually beat the liquid into the mascarpone.

Pour the milk into another saucepan, sprinkle the gelatin over the surface, then heat gently until the gelatin has dissolved. Stir the gelatin-milk into the cream and mascarpone mixture, then strain into a small pitcher.

Pour the cream into the chilled cheesecake crusts and chill for several hours or until set. Remove from the refrigerator 30 minutes before serving.

This cheesecake is the ideal finale to a dinner party—bananas and hazelnuts, topped with pieces of caramel, always make a great combination. Serve with a delicious Toffee Caramel Sauce or even Hot Fudge Sauce (page 62).

banana caramel cheesecake

1½ recipes Nutty Cookie Crumb Base (page 10), made with hazelnuts

Toffee Caramel Sauce (page 62), to serve

Filling

½ cup superfine sugar, plus ½ cup extra for the caramel shards

1 package cream cheese, 8 oz.

2 large eggs, separated

⅔ cup sour cream or crème fraîche

3 ripe medium bananas

finely grated zest and juice of 1 unwaxed lemon

2 tablespoons powdered gelatin

3 oz. chopped toasted hazelnuts, about ½ cup

a false-bottom round cake pan or springform cake pan, 9 inches diameter, greased

a large piece of aluminum foil, oiled

Serves 6–8

Press the crumb mixture evenly over the base of the prepared cake pan, then chill until required. Put the sugar into a saucepan with 6 tablespoons water. Stir to dissolve, then heat slowly until completely dissolved. Have another ⅔ cup water ready. Bring the sugar syrup to a boil, then boil hard until it turns to an amber caramel. Quickly pour in the water—take care, because it will splutter. Stir over gentle heat until the caramel dissolves again, then boil hard until thick and syrupy. Let cool completely.

Put the cream cheese in a bowl and, using a wooden spoon or electric hand mixer, beat until softened. Beat in the egg yolks and sour cream or crème fraîche. Put the bananas into another bowl and mash with a fork. Beat in the lemon zest and juice, then the cheese mixture. Stir in the cold caramel syrup.

Put the gelatin and water in a small heatproof bowl, let sit for 5 minutes, then set over a saucepan of hot water and stir until the gelatin has dissolved. Beat the gelatin into the banana mixture. Set aside until the mixture is on the point of setting (starting to set and thicken).

Put the egg whites into a spotlessly clean, grease-free bowl and beat until soft peaks form, then gently fold into the banana cheese mixture. Pour the mixture into the prepared cake pan and level the surface. Sprinkle with the chopped nuts and chill for 3–4 hours or until set.

To make the caramel shards, sprinkle the sugar lightly over the oiled foil, put under a preheated broiler, and cook until the sugar melts and turns to caramel. Watch carefully or it can burn. Let cool, then break into shards.

Remove the cheesecake from the pan and transfer to a serving plate. Decorate with the caramel shards and serve with toffee caramel sauce.

A wicked, silky smooth, uncooked cheesecake for a summer's day. Serve with a strawberry sauce laced with a little balsamic vinegar to bring out the flavor of the berries and to cut through the richness of the cheesecake.

strawberry and white marshmallow cheesecake

1 recipe Cookie Crumb Base (page 10)

1 recipe Strawberry Sauce (page 63), to serve

Filling

9 oz. mini white marshmallows

2 oz. white chocolate, grated

¼ cup milk

1 envelope powdered gelatin

8 oz. cottage cheese, 1 cup

1 vanilla bean

½ cup sugar

½ cup sour cream

2 egg whites

12 oz. small fresh strawberries, hulled and halved

a springform cake pan or false-bottom cake pan, 8 inches diameter, lined

Serves 6

Press the cookie crumb mixture into the base of the prepared cake pan (using a potato masher helps to flatten the crumb base evenly), then chill until required.

To make the filling, put 7 oz. of the marshmallows and the white chocolate into a heavy saucepan, add the milk and stir over very gentle heat until the marshmallows and chocolate have melted. Remove from the heat. Put the gelatin and ⅓ cup water in a small heatproof bowl, let sit for 5 minutes, then set over a saucepan of hot water and stir until the gelatin has dissolved.

Put the cottage cheese in a large bowl, and using a wooden spoon or electric hand mixer, beat until softened. Split the vanilla bean and scrape out the seeds with the tip of a knife, then beat into the cheese with ¼ cup of the sugar, the melted marshmallow mixture, and sour cream. Beat the gelatin into the cottage cheese mixture, then chill for 15–20 minutes until it starts to thicken (this can happen quite quickly), but does not set.

Put the egg whites into a spotlessly clean, grease-free bowl and beat until stiff but not dry, then beat in the remaining sugar, gradually, spoonful by spoonful, beating until thick after each addition. Gently fold into the cottage cheese mixture. Spoon the mixture into the prepared pan and shake the pan gently to level the surface. Sprinkle the remaining marshmallows over the top—they should completely cover the top. Chill for 3–4 hours or until set.

Carefully remove the cheesecake from the pan. Remove the paper and transfer to a serving plate. Spoon the halved strawberries around the cheesecake and serve with the sauce.

This is a cheesecake inspired by a dessert my mother used to make for special occasions and parties when I was a child—we loved it. Adding cream cheese to the original mixture makes it very luxurious. This version is made upside down, so that when inverted, it has fresh raspberries set into the top.

raspberry fluff cheesecake

about 24 ladyfingers

Filling

1 lb. fresh raspberries

2 tablespoons raspberry and cranberry juice, or just cranberry juice

1 package cream cheese, 8 oz.

½ cup sugar

1 package raspberry Jell-O, prepared according to the instructions on the package

¾ cup evaporated milk

2 extra-large egg whites

a springform cake pan, 10 inches diameter, lined in the bottom and sides with nonstick parchment paper

Serves 10–12

Line the base and sides of the pan with nonstick parchment paper, making sure it doesn't protrude above the edge of the pan. Arrange 10 oz. of the raspberries in a thick layer in the bottom of the pan. Chill.

Put the fruit juice and the remaining raspberries in a small saucepan, bring to a boil, then simmer for 2–3 minutes. Pass through a fine-mesh sieve (don't worry if a few seeds push through) to make a purée. Cool completely.

Put the cream cheese and half of the sugar in a bowl and beat to soften. Gradually beat in the cold raspberry purée.

Cut up the set Jell-O, then put in a saucepan with the evaporated milk. Heat gently, stirring until it dissolves. Cool slightly, then gradually stir into the cheese mixture. Beat the egg whites until stiff, then gradually beat in the remaining sugar until the mixture is until stiff and meringue-like.

Beat 2 large spoonfuls into the cheese and raspberry mixture, then carefully fold in the rest, making sure there are no large pockets of meringue.

Quickly spoon the mixture into the pan on top of the layer of raspberries. Tap the pan gently on the work surface to settle the mixture. Carefully arrange ladyfingers on top of the mixture, trimming to fit. Press in very lightly just to make sure it is touching the whole surface. Chill for 2–3 hours until set.

To serve, invert the pan onto a serving plate and release the spring. Remove the ring and base. Carefully remove the paper from the sides and top and replace any raspberries that may have fallen. Return to the refrigerator until ready to serve.

Cookie Crumb Base

1 stick unsalted butter

2 tablespoons brown sugar

8 oz. chocolate wafers, finely crushed

Filling

1½ packages cream cheese, 8 oz. each

3 large eggs, separated

½ cup sugar

1 teaspoon vanilla extract

1 cup heavy cream

3 envelopes powdered gelatin

Raspberry Ripple

8 oz. fresh or frozen raspberries

¼ cup sugar

Chocolate Ripple

2 oz. semi-sweet chocolate

2 tablespoons heavy cream

a false-bottom deep cake pan, 8 inches diameter, greased and lined

Serves 8

This creamy cheesecake holds rivulets of real raspberry and chocolate sauces in a crisp chocolate cookie case. Alternatively, if your time is limited, you could fold fresh raspberries and grated chocolate into the cheese mixture instead of the sauces.

raspberry and chocolate ripple cheesecake

Put the butter and sugar in a saucepan, melt over gentle heat, then stir in the cookie crumbs. Press the crumb mixture evenly over the base and up the sides of the prepared cake pan. Chill for at least 30 minutes.

Put the cream cheese in a large bowl and, using a wooden spoon or electric hand mixer, beat until softened. Beat in the egg yolks and half the sugar, the vanilla extract, and cream.

Put the gelatin and 2 tablespoons water in a small heatproof bowl set over a saucepan of hot water, and stir occasionally until the the gelatin has dissolved. Keep it warm. To make the raspberry ripple, put the raspberries and sugar in a saucepan and gently heat until the sugar dissolves. Boil for 1 minute until slightly thickened. Press through a fine-mesh sieve and let cool. To make the chocolate ripple, put the chocolate and cream in another saucepan, heat until the chocolate has melted, then stir well and let cool until just warm, but still pourable. Beat the gelatin into the cheese mixture.

Put the egg whites in a spotlessly clean, grease-free bowl, whisk until stiff but not dry, then whisk in the remaining sugar, gradually, spoonful by spoonful, whisking until thick after each addition. Beat 2 spoonfuls of the meringue into the cheese mixture, then quickly fold in the rest. Put small spoonfuls of mixture in the base of the crust so that they join up, then pour the raspberry and chocolate sauces in between the spoonfuls of mixture. Spoon over the remaining cheese mixture and pour again (keep any remaining sauces to serve). Swirl the mixtures together with a skewer to produce a ripple effect. Give the pan a shake to settle the mixture and chill for 2–4 hours until set. To serve, remove the cake from the pan and carefully peel off the paper. Serve in thin slices with any extra sauces.

I have based this on a beautiful dessert often seen in French pâtisseries. The pink base is covered by a deep purple-red, shiny "lake" of set black currant purée.

blackberry lake cheesecake

1 medium ready-made poundcake, about 9 inches diameter

Filling

8 oz. fresh or frozen blackberries

½ cup plus 1 tablespoon sugar

¼ cup crème de cassis

1½ packages cream cheese, 8 oz. each

2 large eggs, separated

1 cup heavy cream

1 envelope powdered gelatin

Lake Topping

¼ cup blackcurrant syrup

1 teaspoon powdered gelatin

fresh blackberries, dusted with confectioners' sugar, to decorate

a springform cake pan, 9 inches diameter, oiled

Serves 8

Carefully cut the cake in half horizontally. Wrap and freeze one half for use another time. Put the base of the springform pan on top of the cake and cut around to fit the pan. Set aside. Arrange the cake in the bottom of the prepared pan.

Put the fruit in a saucepan with the sugar. Bring to a boil and simmer for 5 minutes. Transfer the fruit to a blender, add the crème de cassis, and work until smooth. Press through a fine-mesh sieve to remove the seeds and set aside the purée. Let cool completely. Set aside 2 tablespoons to make the glaze.

Put the cream cheese, egg yolks, and cream in a bowl and, using a wooden spoon or electric hand mixer, beat well, then stir in the purée. Put the gelatin and ⅓ cup water in a small heatproof bowl and let sit for 5 minutes. Set the bowl over a saucepan of hot water, stir gently until the gelatin has dissolved, then stir into the cheese mixture. Put the egg whites in a spotlessly clean, grease-free bowl, beat until stiff but not dry, then fold into the mixture. Pour into the prepared pan and level the surface. Chill for 3–4 hours until firm.

To make the lake topping, put the ¼ cup blackcurrant syrup, the reserved blackberry purée, and the gelatin in a small saucepan and mix well. Heat until the gelatin has dissolved, then cool until almost cold and just turning to syrup. Carefully pour over the surface of the cheesecake, making sure it covers the top. Chill for a further 1 hour. Carefully remove from the pan and set on a serving plate. Decorate with sugared berries and serve.

2 recipes Cookie Crumb Base (page 10), made with almond macaroons

edible flower petals, such as marigolds, for sprinkling (optional)

Candied Needleshreds of Orange Zest (optional)

2 unwaxed oranges

¼ cup superfine sugar

Filling

4 large eggs, separated

½ cup sugar

finely grated zest and juice of 2 unwaxed oranges

2 envelopes powdered gelatin

12 oz. cottage cheese, strained

1¼ cups heavy cream

2 tablespoons orange flower water (optional)

8 false-bottom tartlet tins, 3½ inches diameter, ¾ inch deep

a large baking tray

Serves 8

These little cheesecakes are an updated version of an old English recipe often served in little glasses or cups. Using cottage cheese gives a grainy texture and the orange flower water a wonderful light orange flavor.

orange blossom cheesecakes

Press the crumb mixture neatly into the base and sides of the tartlet pans. Set on a large baking tray and chill until required.

Put the egg yolks, sugar, orange zest, and juice in a small heatproof bowl and set over a saucepan of simmering water. Using an electric hand mixer, beat until thick and foamy—do not let it get too hot or the mixture will scramble. Remove from the heat and beat until cold.

Put the gelatin and ⅓ cup water in another small heatproof bowl and let sit for 5 minutes. Set the bowl over a saucepan of hot water and stir gently until the gelatin has dissolved.

Put the strained cottage cheese in a large bowl with the cream and orange flower water, if using. Using a wooden spoon or electric hand mixer, beat lightly, then stir in the melted gelatin. Gently fold in the beaten egg mixture and set aside in a cool place until on the point of setting. Spoon the setting mixture into the tartlet crusts to look like a pile of clouds. Chill for 2–3 hours until set.

If making the needleshreds, remove the zest from the oranges with a sharp potato peeler (removing any bitter white pith with a knife afterwards). Cut the zest into long fine needleshreds. Boil the shreds for 1 minute, then refresh in cold water. Put the sugar and ½ cup water in a small saucepan and stir until dissolved. Add the shreds and bring to a rolling boil for 2–3 minutes, then strain and put on a plate to cool. Before they cool too much, separate them so that they don't stick together.

Serve the cheesecake sprinkled with a few edible flower petals or Orange Needleshreds, if using.

A cheesecake for a buffet party. It bursts with juicy pieces of tangerine, and is very refreshing after a meal. For a special occasion, try using tangerines or clementines ready-prepared in liqueur and sugar syrup, available from gourmet stores.

tangerine and chocolate cheesecake

Base

1 stick unsalted butter

8 oz. chocolate wafers, crushed

Filling

8 unwaxed tangerines

3 envelopes powdered gelatin

2 packages mascarpone or cream cheese, 8 oz. each

4 large eggs, separated

1 cup sugar

1¼ cups sour cream or crème fraîche

3 tablespoons Cointreau or Grand Marnier

swirls of cream, piped chocolate decorations, and tangerine segments half-dipped in chocolate, to decorate

a springform cake pan, 10 inches diameter, lined

Serves 12

Put the butter in a small saucepan, melt over gentle heat, then stir in the cookie crumbs. Press evenly into the base of the prepared cake pan and chill for 30 minutes.

Finely grate the zest of 2 tangerines and set aside. Squeeze the juice from 4 of the tangerines and pour into a small saucepan. Sprinkle with the gelatin and let sit for 10 minutes. Remove the flesh from the segments of the remaining tangerines and chop it coarsely.

Put the mascarpone in a large bowl and, using a wooden spoon or electric hand mixer, beat until softened. Beat in the egg yolks, ½ cup of the sugar, the sour cream or crème fraîche, and liqueur. Heat the gelatin mixture slowly until dissolved, then stir into the cheese mixture. Fold in the tangerine zest and chopped tangerines.

Put the egg whites in a spotlessly clean, grease-free bowl, beat until stiff, then gradually beat in the remaining sugar. Fold into the cheese mixture and spoon into the cake pan. Level the surface and chill for 3–4 hours until set.

Carefully remove the cheesecake from the pan and set on a serving plate. Decorate with swirls of cream topped with chocolate decorations and chocolate-dipped tangerine segments. Alternatively, pipe an irregular criss-cross pattern over the top of the cake with a little melted chocolate.

The subtle combination of coconut and lychee makes these individual cheesecakes irresistible.

lychee and coconut cheesecakes

1½ recipes Cookie Crumb Base (page 10), made with ginger cookies

thinly sliced kiwifruit, toasted shaved coconut, and finely sliced candied ginger, to decorate

Filling

2 unwaxed oranges

¼ cup superfine sugar

½ cup coconut cream

⅓ cup sweet dessert wine, such as Moscatel de Valencia

1 tablespoon ground ginger

2 teaspoons powdered gelatin

24 fresh or canned lychees

5 tablespoons coconut liqueur, such as Malibu

1¼ cups mascarpone

3 tablespoons chopped candied ginger

2 large egg whites

¼ cup sugar

6 false-bottom tartlet pans, about 4 inches diameter

Serves 6

Press the crumb mixture into the bases and sides of the tartlet pans. Chill in the refrigerator until required.

Put coconut in a saucepan with the sweet wine and gelatin. Heat very gently until the coconut has melted. Do not boil. Stir well and pour into a blender.

If using fresh lychees, peel and pit them, then put the flesh into the blender. Add the coconut liqueur and blend until smooth.

Put the mascarpone in a large bowl and, using a wooden spoon or electric hand mixer, beat until softened, then gradually beat the purée into the cheese. Stir in the ground ginger.

Put the egg whites in a spotlessly clean, grease-free bowl, beat until stiff but not dry, then beat in the sugar, gradually, spoonful by spoonful, beating until thick after each addition. Beat 2 spoonfuls of the egg white mixture into the cheese mixture, then fold in the rest. Spoon the filling into the prepared pans and level the surface. Chill in the refrigerator for at least 30 minutes.

Decorate with the kiwifruit, coconut, and ginger, then serve.

The truly tropical flavour of coconut, mango, and passionfruit are given a lift with coconut liqueur and orange and lime juice.

coconut cheesecake
with mango and passionfruit sauce

1 recipe Cookie Crumb Base (page 10)

Filling

1¾ cups canned coconut milk

1 vanilla bean

1 cup milk

4 large egg yolks

½ cup plus 2 tablespoons sugar

2 tablespoons powdered gelatin

⅔ cup mascarpone

3 tablespoons coconut liqueur

Sauce

1 large ripe mango, about 1 lb.

freshly squeezed juice of 1 orange

freshly squeezed juice of 1 lime

2 ripe wrinkled passionfruit

confectioners' sugar, to taste

6 deep metal rings, 2½ inches diameter, about 2 inches deep, with capacity of ½ cup, oiled (I use washed and dried food cans, opened at each end)

a baking sheet with sides

Serves 6

Stand the prepared rings on a baking sheet and press a layer of the crumb mixture into the base of each one. Chill. Put the coconut milk into a non-aluminum saucepan (otherwise it will discolor) and beat well. Split the vanilla bean lengthwise and scrape the black seeds into the coconut milk. Stir in the milk, heat to boiling point, then remove from the heat.

Put the egg yolks and sugar in a bowl and beat until pale and fluffy. Pour on the scalded coconut milk and stir well. Return to the saucepan and cook over gentle heat, stirring, until thickened like heavy cream. Do not boil, otherwise it will curdle. This will take about 15 minutes. Strain this custard into a bowl, cover with damp wax paper, and cool. Put the gelatin and ¼ cup cold water in a small heatproof bowl and set aside for 5 minutes. Set the bowl over a saucepan of simmering water until dissolved. Stir occasionally, then cool slightly. Put the mascarpone in a second bowl and beat in the liqueur to loosen it, then beat in the custard. Stir the gelatin into the cheese mixture. Chill for 15–20 minutes until the custard starts to thicken slightly. Pour into the rings and chill for 2–3 hours until set.

To make the sauce, peel the mango and cut the flesh away from the seed. Put in a blender with the orange and lime juice, blend until smooth, then press through a fine-mesh sieve into a bowl. Halve the passionfruit, scoop out the seeds, and stir them into the sauce. Add confectioners' sugar to taste. If the sauce is a little too thick, add more orange juice. Chill.

To serve, loosen the cheesecakes, slide each one onto a plate, remove the rings, and spoon a little sauce over the top.

A dense cheesecake to serve with coffee after dinner. It couldn't be any easier to make. You may add any liqueur you like, but my preference is for rum. Serve in thin slices, straight from the refrigerator so that it is as cool and firm as possible.

chocolate macaroon truffle cheesecake

1 recipe Chocolate Crumb Base (page 10)

Filling

8 oz. bittersweet chocolate

10 oz. cream cheese

½ cup brown sugar

¼ cup dark rum

4 oz. macaroons, finely crushed

unsweetened cocoa powder, sifted, for dusting

a false-bottom shallow cake pan, 9 inches diameter

Serves 6–8

Press the crumb mixture thinly (you may not have to use it all) over the base of the cake pan and chill until required.

Break the chocolate into small, even pieces and put in a small heatproof bowl set over a saucepan of hot water. Stir constantly over low heat, until the chocolate has melted, then set aside.

Put the cream cheese in a large bowl and, using a wooden spoon or electric hand mixer, beat until softened. Beat in the sugar and rum, then stir in the melted chocolate and crushed macaroons. Spoon into the pan and level the surface as neatly as possible. Chill for 1–2 hours.

When firm, dust the top with a thin layer of cocoa powder. Carefully remove from the pan (you may like to warm the sides of the pan to release the cheesecake), set on a large plate, and serve.

A semifreddo is a dessert that is half frozen to give it a slightly thickened, creamy texture. Ricotta and mascarpone are sweetened, laced with rum and Tía María, and flavored with pulverized Italian coffee and grated chocolate to give an interesting texture. You must buy espresso coffee that is very finely ground or it will taste gritty!

coffee ricotta semifreddo cheesecake

1½ recipes Chocolate Crumb Base (page 10)

chocolate shards or curls, made from 8 oz. semi-sweet chocolate, melted, to decorate

confectioners' sugar, for dusting

whipped cream, to serve (optional)

Filling

12 oz. ricotta cheese, at room temperature

12 oz. mascarpone, at room temperature

1 tablespoon dark rum

3 tablespoons coffee liqueur, such as Tía María

1 teaspoon vanilla extract

¼ cup confectioners' sugar

8 oz. grated bittersweet chocolate

2 tablespoons finely ground espresso Italian roast coffee

a springform cake pan, 10 inches diameter, lined

Serves 6–8

Press the crumb mixture into the base of the cake pan. (Using a potato masher helps to flatten the crumb base evenly.) Chill until required.

Press the ricotta cheese through a fine-mesh sieve into a bowl, then beat in the mascarpone with a wooden spoon. (Do not attempt to do this in a food processor, or the mixture will be too runny.)

Beat in the rum, coffee liqueur, vanilla extract, and sugar, then fold in the grated chocolate and ground coffee leaving the mixture very streaky. Carefully spoon into the prepared pan, leaving the surface coarse.

Put into the freezer for about 2 hours until just frozen, not rock solid. The dessert should be only just frozen or very chilled. If too hard, transfer to the refrigerator 30 minutes before serving to soften slightly.

To serve, unmold, remove the paper, and set on a large serving plate. Use a knife to cut through very cold semi-sweet chocolate to make spiky shards, then use to cover the surface of the cheesecake. Alternatively, make chocolate curls. Spread melted chocolate on a marble slab to a depth of ⅛ inch. When just set, draw a fine-bladed knife across the chocolate at a 45-degree angle to shave off curls. Dust with confectioners' sugar and serve with a spoonful of whipped cream, if using.

sauces

chocolate sauce

3 oz. best-quality bittersweet
chocolate

½ cup sugar

1 teaspoon unsweetened
cocoa powder

1 teaspoon vanilla extract

Makes about 1½ cups

Break the chocolate into small,
even pieces and put in a small
heavy saucepan. Add the sugar,
cocoa, and 1¼ cups water. Heat
gently, stirring occasionally, until
the chocolate has melted. Bring
to a boil and simmer for 15–20
minutes until syrupy and very
glossy.

Remove from the heat, stir in the
vanilla extract, then let cool.
Reheat slowly to serve.

hot fudge sauce

2 oz. bittersweet chocolate

1 tablespoon unsalted butter

2 tablespoons light corn syrup

¾ cup brown sugar

1 teaspoon vanilla extract

Makes about 1 cup

Break the chocolate into
small, even pieces and put in
a medium bowl set over a
saucepan of barely simmering
water. Leave for 10 minutes
until completely melted, then
stir in the butter. Add ⅓ cup
boiling water, stir well, then
stir in the corn syrup and
sugar.

Transfer to a small saucepan,
bring to a boil, turn the heat
down, and leave at the lowest
simmer for 5 minutes.
Remove from the heat
immediately and stir in the
vanilla. Keep warm over the
hot water—it will set as it
cools. It can be remelted
easily over gentle heat.

taffy caramel sauce

¼ cup light corn syrup

2 tablespoons brown sugar

1 tablespoon unsalted butter

⅔ cup heavy cream

freshly squeezed juice of ½ large lemon

Makes about 1¼ cups

Put the corn syrup, sugar, and butter
in a medium saucepan, heat over
gentle heat until dissolved, then boil
until a rich golden brown color.

Remove the saucepan from the heat,
add ⅔ cup water, return to the heat,
and stir until dissolved. Pour in the
cream and lemon juice, then boil until
syrupy. Let cool. This sauce is best
served warm.

strawberry sauce

1 lb. fresh strawberries

2 tablespoons confectioners' sugar

1 tablespoon balsamic vinegar

Makes about 1¼ cups

Hull and halve the strawberries, then put them in a small saucepan with the confectioners' sugar and 3 tablespoons water. Heat slowly until the juices start to run, then transfer to a blender or food processor, add the balsamic vinegar, and purée until smooth. If you prefer, press the sauce through a fine-mesh sieve to remove the seeds. Pour into a small bowl, cover with plastic wrap and chill until required.

Variation Make raspberry sauce the same way, but substitute raspberry vinegar for the balsamic vinegar—it adds an elegant sharp note to the sauce.

mascarpone cream

2 cups mascarpone or heavy cream

3 tablespoons confectioners' sugar

½ cup Italian Vin Santo or Marsala wine

Makes about 2½ cups

Put the mascarpone, sugar, and Vin Santo in a large bowl and, using an electric hand mixer or balloon whisk, beat until soft peaks form. Chill until required.

lemon syllabub cream

finely grated zest and juice of 1 unwaxed lemon

⅓ cup Madeira wine or sherry

⅔ cup dry white wine, Madeira, or sherry

freshly grated nutmeg

2 cups heavy cream

confectioners' sugar, to taste

Makes about 3 cups

Put the lemon zest in a bowl with the Madeira, wine, and grated nutmeg. Let macerate for at least 1 hour. Strain into another bowl.

Put the cream and confectioners' sugar to taste in another bowl, and using an electric hand mixer or balloon whisk, beat until just starting to thicken, then gradually beat in the flavored wine until the mixture forms soft peaks. Use immediately otherwise it will separate.

index

conversion charts

Weights and measures have been rounded up or down slightly to make measuring easier.

Volume equivalents:

American	Metric	Imperial
1 teaspoon	5 ml	
1 tablespoon	15 ml	
¼ cup	60 ml	2 fl.oz.
⅓ cup	75 ml	2½ fl.oz.
½ cup	125 ml	4 fl.oz.
⅔ cup	150 ml	5 fl.oz. (¼ pint)
¾ cup	175 ml	6 fl.oz.
1 cup	250 ml	8 fl.oz.

Weight equivalents: **Measurements:**

Imperial	Metric	Inches	Cm
1 oz.	25 g	¼ inch	5 mm
2 oz.	50 g	½ inch	1 cm
3 oz.	75 g	¾ inch	1.5 cm
4 oz.	125 g	1 inch	2.5 cm
5 oz.	150 g	2 inches	5 cm
6 oz.	175 g	3 inches	7 cm
7 oz.	200 g	4 inches	10 cm
8 oz. (½ lb.)	250 g	5 inches	12 cm
9 oz.	275 g	6 inches	15 cm
10 oz.	300 g	7 inches	18 cm
11 oz.	325 g	8 inches	20 cm
12 oz.	375 g	9 inches	23 cm
13 oz.	400 g	10 inches	25 cm
14 oz.	425 g	11 inches	28 cm
15 oz.	475 g	12 inches	30 cm
16 oz. (1 lb.)	500 g		
2 lb.	1 kg		

Oven temperatures:

110°C	(225°F)	Gas ¼
120°C	(250°F)	Gas ½
140°C	(275°F)	Gas 1
150°C	(300°F)	Gas 2
160°C	(325°F)	Gas 3
180°C	(350°F)	Gas 4
190°C	(375°F)	Gas 5
200°C	(400°F)	Gas 6
220°C	(425°F)	Gas 7
230°C	(450°F)	Gas 8
240°C	(475°F)	Gas 9